# A Hundred Words For Grand

First published 2023 by The O'Brien Press Ltd.,
12 Terenure Road East, Rathgar, Dublin 6, D06 HD27, Ireland.
Tel: +353 1 4923333; Fax: +353 1 4922777
E-mail: books@obrien.ie
Website: obrien.ie
The O'Brien Press is a member of Publishing Ireland.

ISBN: 978-1-78849-438-0

10 9 8 7 6 5 4 3 2 1
27 26 25 24 23

Layout and design: The O'Brien Press Ltd.

Printed and bound by Hussar Books, Poland.
The paper in this book is produced using pulp from managed forests.

Published in:

# A Hundred Words For Grand

## The little book of Irish chat

Kunak McGann

THE O'BRIEN PRESS
DUBLIN

# OPENERS &
# CLOSERS

Alright, bud? / Anything strange or startlin'? / 'Bout ye? / How's she cuttin'? / How's she hangin'? / How's the form? / Howya? / Howya gettin' on? / Story, horse? / What are ye at? / What's the craic? / Well?

*How are you?*

Why have one way of asking how someone is when you can have a dozen? Different phrases are more popular in different parts of the country, but for the most part you can just choose one and dive in!

**Usage:** 'Ah janey, I haven't seen you in ages. What's the craic?'
'Divil a bit, you know yourself.'

# Divil a bit / Not a bother / Sure, I'm grand / You know yourself

*I'm fine, thanks for asking.*

The Irish tradition, when asked how you are, is to reassure your interrogator that all is well. This is no time for raw emotion or sob stories; quiet stoicism is what you're looking for here.

**Usage:** 'I heard your house was flooded, your car packed in, and your wife left you. Howya gettin' on?'
'Sure, I'm grand.'

# C'mere to me

*Attention seeker.*

When an Irish person, especially a Dub, starts a conversation off with this, you may settle in for a long one. With a touch of the conspiratorial, you're about to be told a secret, some salacious gossip, or a tale that may well be embellished to elicit maximum shock. Prepare your wide eyes and best gasp.

**Usage:** 'C'mere to me, did you hear who died?'

# A cup in your hand

*Irish hospitality.*

Ours is a nation renowned for extending a warm welcome, so it's no surprise that when visiting friends or family here, they'll never leave you empty-handed — a cup of tea is always in order. Tea's not your thing? Refuse at your peril.

**Usage**: 'Won't you come in? Ah, you'll have a cup in your hand.'

# Wet the tea

*Culinary command.*

The Irish are some of the largest consumers of tea in the world (second only to the Turkish), and we take it pretty seriously. If someone asks you to 'wet the tea', you should throw a few teabags in the teapot and add boiling water. Then allow it to brew for maximum colour and flavour – the darker the better, so that adding milk only turns it a sort of reddish-orange. Yum.

**Usage:** 'Make yourself useful and go wet the tea, would ya? I fancy a cup of scald.'

# Thanks a million

*Words of appreciation.*

When 'thanks a lot' just isn't effusive enough. This one is thought to originate in the Irish phrase *Go raibh míle maith agat*, meaning 'a thousand good things to you'. Watch out for the tone of delivery though; a good dollop of sarcasm can flip it to mean the opposite: 'Thanks *a million*' (accompanied by a theatrical eye roll).

**Usage:** 'A jumbo breakfast roll and red lemonade? My favourite! Thanks a million.'

# Take it handy

*Friendly leave-taking.*

A nice little substitute for 'Take it easy' or 'See you later', this is a genial way of bidding someone farewell. Can also be a reminder to someone not to get too carried away in whatever they're off to next. Steady, there!

**Usage:** 'I hear you're signed up for the Dublin Marathon in October. Take it handy, will ya?'

# Sure lookit / Sure listen

*Verbal shrug.*

Two common phrases that, let's face it, no-one truly understands. Used to indicate the end of an exchange and often spoken in a tone of resignation — a holding up of your hands and a 'let's leave it at that' — or a non-committal response to a story: 'What can you do?'

**Usage:** 'Ah sure lookit, isn't that it?'
''Tis an' all.'

# Bye, bye, bye, bye, bye

*Drawn-out farewell.*

Nobody really knows why, but when using the phone, the Irish are incapable of saying 'bye' just the once. Instead, there's a string of them — or even more than one string. In fact, if someone only offers one 'bye' when taking their leave of you, it's time to start questioning your friendship.

**Usage:** 'Bye. Bye, bye. Bye, bye, bye. Bye, bye, bye, bye, bye.'

SMALL TALK

# Grand

*It's complicated.*

'Grand' can mean anything from 'ok' or 'fine' right down to 'not well at all' or 'truly awful', and context and tone are everything. It's also incredibly adaptable: a person can feel 'grand, thanks' or have 'got on grand'; the day can be 'a grand soft one' or have a 'grand stretch' in it. And when offering someone something, 'grand' implies acceptance while both 'I'm grand' and 'you're grand' are polite refusals. Truly fluent use of the word requires extensive immersion in Irish culture.

**Usage:** 'Don't be worrying about it. It'll all be GRAND.'

# I will, yea

*I will not.*

Another example of the charming Irish habit of saying one thing and meaning the opposite. Delivered with a straight face, a characteristic wry tone and perhaps a raised eyebrow, this little phrase means someone has no intention whatsoever of helping you out. You may forget it.

**Usage:** 'Sit around waiting 'til you're ready to be collected? I will, yea.'

# Awful / Fierce / Pure / Quare / Shocking / Terrible

*Very very.*

Sometimes adding 'very' just isn't strong enough, and when emphasis is called for, the Irish have a unique and colourful range of intensifiers. Pair them with any adjective you like to really give your descriptions that extra punch.

**Usage:** 'Get me a drink, would you? I'm quare thirsty.'

# Leppin'

*Bleedin' starving.*

This word stems from the Irish pronunciation of 'leaping', but this particular definition comes from the longer phrase 'leppin' with the hunger'. Nonsensical but dramatic, like all the best Irish slang.

**Usage:** 'I am absolutely leppin'. I could eat a cow between two bread vans.'

# Go away outta that / Would ya stop?

*Gentle remonstration.*

An expression of disbelief or refusal, calling on someone not to be so ridiculous or to stop joking. It can also double as a good deflection when someone gives you a compliment (and there's nothing that embarrasses the Irish like a nice compliment).

**Usage:** 'This old thing? Would you go away outta that!'

# Whisht

*Hush!*

A charming way of telling someone to keep it down, please. Can also be incorporated into the phrase 'houl your whisht' (hold your whisht). Often used by harried parents or teachers with increasing insistence as the decibels rise around them.

**Usage:** 'Would ye ever whisht? I can't hear myself think!'

# No bodge

*No bother.*

This little gem comes from the British slang word 'bodge', to botch something. The Irish have adapted it to 'no bodge', meaning no hassle, no worries. A phrase of friendly reassurance.

**Usage**: 'I'm after putting those messages in the press for you. It was no bodge at all.'

# Yoke

*Thingamajig.*

When you can't remember the name of something, that's where 'yoke' comes in as an excellent substitute for pretty much any 'thing'. It can also be used for a person, particularly someone outrageous or unconventional: a 'mad yoke'.

**Usage:** 'Would you ever give me that yoke there? No, not that yoke. The other yoke.'

# Fooster

*Multi-purpose verb.*

From the Irish word *fústar*, meaning fuss/ fidgetiness, this is a tricky one to pin down. To fiddle about or procrastinate, it can also mean to dig around looking for something. You can fooster with something, over something, or just fooster around or about. Take your pick of prepositions.

**Usage**: 'Kids, would ya stop foostering around and just get in the car?'

# Scarlet / Morto

*Mortified.*

Red-faced with embarrassment, 'scarlet'
is particularly popular in Dublin. Used
interchangeably with 'morto' for the most
humiliating of situations.

**Usage:** 'I can't believe you just did that. I'm
scarlet for you and scarlet for yer ma for
having you.'

# Janey mac

*Expression of surprise.*

A phrase that goes back a long way, some say even as far back as Fionn Mac Cumhaill and his original name, Deimne (Deimne Mac). It also became part of a popular children's rhyme, 'Janey mac, me shirt is black'. But mostly, it's an alternative to 'Jesus, Mary and Joseph' that's safe to say in front of even the most devout relatives.

**Usage:** 'Janey mac! How did you get yourself into that state?'

# Sweet mother of Divine / Jesus, Mary and Joseph

*A cry to the heavens.*

Steeped as our culture has been in the Catholic religion, it's no wonder that we often call out not just to God himself but to his whole family tree. These pious ejaculations can be uttered in a tone of shock or sheer exasperation. When the situation is absolutely dire, we are even known to throw in 'and the wee donkey'.

**Usage:** 'Jesus, Mary and Joseph, would the lot of ye ever pipe down?'

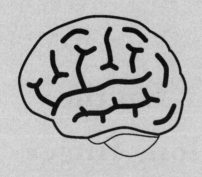

# WORDS OF
# WISDOM

# On the
# long finger

*Eventually.*

This phrase derives from an Irish proverb, *Cuir gach rud ar an mhéar fhada agus beidh an mhéar fhada róghairid ar ball*, meaning 'If you put everything on the long finger, the long finger will be too short in time'. If there's a people that know how to put something on the long finger, it's the Irish, alright.

**Usage:** 'It's not on the long finger, I swear. I'll get to it. You don't have to remind me every six months.'

# Chancing your arm

*Taking a gamble.*

Satisfyingly, this phrase has very literal origins. In 1492, the Butlers and the FitzGeralds weren't getting on. When the two clans had a stand-off at St. Patrick's Cathedral, Gerald FitzGerald had a hole cut in a door so he could put his arm through and offer his handshake. And the Irish have been happily chancing their arms ever since.

**Usage:** 'Do you really know anything about performing abdominal surgery, or are you just chancing your arm?'

# Like hen's teeth

*Very rare.*

The dentistry of poultry seems a strange thing to base a phrase on, but right enough, you'd have to make your way through A LOT of hens before you find one with a tooth. For anyone with time on their hands.

**Usage:** 'Around here, an eligible bachelor with good road frontage is as rare as hen's teeth.'

# Far from that you were raised

*Having notions.*

Often slated as a nation of begrudgers, the Irish are quick to point out when you've gotten above your station and are turning your back on the family that raised you. This little phrase is designed to bring you back down to earth with a bump.

**Usage:** 'Avocado on sourdough and an oat milk latte for brunch? 'Tis far from that you were raised.'

# Not a
# bull's notion

*Not a feckin' clue.*

It's always nice to hear an Irish expression with an agricultural spin, although it's not quite clear why the bull has been singled out from other farming stock for his dubious comprehension skills. This phrase is always used in the negative: you'll never hear about someone who DOES have a bull's notion.

**Usage:** 'Any idea where I can score myself a pair of tickets for the All-Ireland final? I haven't a bull's notion where to start.'

# Didn't lick it off a stone

*It runs in the family.*

The Irish are wading into the 'nature vs nurture' debate with this one, a charming way of saying that someone has picked up a particular character trait from one of their parents. What the rest of the world means by 'the apple never falls far from the tree'.

**Usage:** 'Have you ever met his mother? It's not off the stones he licked it.'

# Put the heart crossways

*Quite the shock.*

When 'you gave me a fright' isn't melodramatic enough, there's putting the heart crossways in someone. A phrase without any medically sound basis.

**Usage:** 'Jaysus, I didn't see you there! You put the heart crossways in me.'

# Up to 90

*Mad busy.*

When someone is 'up to 90', they're absolutely flat out. Does the expression come from miles per hour, a temperature nearing boiling point, or even an elevated heart rate? Who knows? And when you're up to 90, you don't have time to think about it either.

**Usage:** 'When would I have had time to pick up the phone? Haven't I been up to 90 since I got out of bed this morning?'

# Give it a lash

*Have a go.*

A phrase showcasing the Irish can-do attitude: go on and give it some welly. Irish people of a certain age will forever remember the classic song 'Give It a Lash, Jack', released in the midst of the countrywide mania for the 1990 World Cup. Rev it up and here we go!

**Usage**: 'Haven't a clue what I'm at here but feck it, I'll give it a lash!'

# Stall the ball

*Hold your horses.*

This is a lighthearted way of calling on someone to slow down or stop when you need a chance to catch up, on a walk or a conversation. And it has the added bonus of rhyming. Nice.

**Usage:** 'Stall the ball, will ya, lads? I'm not feeling the Mae West.'

# You wouldn't turn a sweet in your mouth

*Absolutely jammers.*

This is a curious phrase meaning that somewhere is so thronged full of people, so jammed to the rafters, that there isn't even room to manoeuvre an iced caramel in your own mouth. Now that's PACKED.

**Usage:** 'An intimate venue, they said. It was so busy you wouldn't turn a sweet in your mouth. There'd be more room in a Trócaire box.'

DROCHAIMSIR

# Soft day, thank God

*Damp salutation.*

You know those days when droplets of rain seem to hang in the sky like a Matrix slow-mo — a lingering mist that permeates everywhere and wets you through in a matter of minutes? That is a soft day, and in Ireland (and particularly the Wesht), it's a good thing. Not just a comment on the weather, the phrase also doubles as a general greeting between locals.

**Usage:** 'Soft day, thank God.'
'It is indeed. A grand soft day.'

# Drizzling / Spitting

*Light sprinkling of rain.*

When the weather hasn't quite descended into all-out pouring rain. Rain you can hardly see looking out through your window, it falls gently to the ground without making too much of a commotion. Stealthy precipitation.

**Usage:** 'Do we have to call off the BBQ this afternoon? Sure it's only spitting. Get the anoraks on, lads!'

# Coming down in sheets / Bucketing / Hammering / Lashing / Pegging it / Pelting / Pouring / Teeming

*Rain, rain, and more rain.*

Given our frequent exposure to inclement weather, it's no surprise that the Irish have a plethora of words for rain – in this case, heavy rain. All of these words and phrases refer to not just a slight smattering of the wet stuff, but a deluge from the heavens. Brolly definitely required.

**Usage:** 'It's pure wet outside. It's absolutely pelting down.'

# Wet rain

*Seems obvious.*

As counterintuitive as it may sound, not all types of rain are as wet as each other. Here in Ireland, 'wet rain' means a soft type of rain — gently falling but still carrying an unexpectedly large amount of moisture. Rain that really does its job well.

**Usage:** 'That's terrible wet rain. Look at you! You're drownded.'

# Dirty-looking sky

*Bad omen.*

Sinister words of foreboding spoken with narrowed eyes, when the utterer strongly suspects that rain is imminent. They usually mean a dark-grey sky full to the brim with alarmingly sodden-looking clouds. For Ireland, can be used every other day then, really.

**Usage:** 'That's a dirty-looking sky up there. I wouldn't stray far.'

# Down for the day /
# A day for the fire

*Soggy prospect.*

When there are puddles as far as the eye can see, it's been raining through the night and will likely be raining through the day too. There's nothing for it but to cancel all outdoor plans and stock up on the firewood. Time to catch up on the box-sets.

**Usage:** 'Into the pyjamas and get that kettle on. It's down for the day.'

Baltic / Bitter out /
Getting the wear out
of the winter coat

*Cold snap.*

Whether your taste runs to understatement or overstatement to describe the cold, the Irish have you covered. 'Bitter out' or 'getting the wear out of the winter coat' for the unassuming. But for those with a flair for the dramatic, it's definitely 'Baltic' — as cold as we imagine it is in a winter Baltic Sea (but aren't really willing to try out).

**Usage:** 'Getting the wear out of the winter coat? Are you joking me? It's bleedin' BALTIC out there!'

# That wind would cut you in half

*Icy expression.*

We all know the type of wind that isn't just cold, it's FREEZING. A cold so bitter on your skin it feels like it's physically cutting through you. It could even be the dreaded north wind your parents always warned you about, blowing straight down from the Arctic. Brrrr.

**Usage:** 'That wind would cut you in half.' 'Not just in half. Quarters.'

# The Big Snow

*Historic event.*

Ireland hasn't really seen a lot of full-on snow in living memory: there was 1963, then 1982, then 2010. But all of them were blown out of the water by the arrival of the Beast from the East and Storm Emma in 2018. Deep snow drifts, widespread electricity cuts and, perhaps the worst hardship of all, not a sliced pan to be found anywhere.

**Usage:** 'Do you remember the Big Snow, when Uncle Seamus's Ford Escort was buried in that ten-foot drift? Took him a week to dig it out.'

# HERE COMES
# THE SUN

# Fierce mild / Roasting

*Nearly too hot.*

Some may think that 'fierce' and 'mild' are opposites, but not the Irish. When the few days of summer arrive and temperatures soar, that's when we alternate the terms 'fierce mild' and 'roasting'. And not necessarily in a complimentary way either.

**Usage:** 'It's fierce mild even in the shade today. I'm sweatin' buckets.'

# Splitting
# the stones

*Rock–breaking heat.*

Coming from the Irish language *ag scoilteadh na gcloch*, this is weather so good that the heat from the sun is literally cracking the stones. That's pretty sunny. And unprecedented, given Ireland's notoriously temperate climate.

**Usage:** 'The sun is splitting the stones out there. Pass me that Factor 50. Quick!'

# I always burn
# first, then tan

*Outright lie.*

Ireland is crammed with people who are deficient in melanin but convinced they are otherwise. Recent years have seen a welcome surge in the use of sun cream, but there are still those who'd rather grit their teeth through the pain of third-degree sunburn and a week of peeling skin. Ugh.

**Usage:** 'Ah yeah, I know my skin is so red it looks radioactive, but I always burn first, then tan.'

# Melting /
# Not able for
# this heat

*Shweatin'.*

The Irish — most of us, at least — are not equipped for extreme sunny weather. While we may moan about the rain, we moan even more about the heat. For the least well-equipped, they can feel like they're literally melting, *Wizard of Oz* witch style. Sure, you'd be glued to the mattress at night.

**Usage:** 'Ah lads, I'm not able for this heat. I'm like a dead dog.'

They're giving it fine
for the week / It's to
break at the weekend

*Weather forecast.*

In the middle of a dry spell, the Irish are always split into two groups: the optimists who relish the thought of a full week of fine weather ahead and the pessimists already dreading the inevitable return of the rain.

**Usage:** 'The Leaving Cert starts on Wednesday. No wonder they're giving it fine for the next two weeks.'

# Why would you go on a foreign holiday?

*Rhetorical question.*

We Irish are convinced there is no better place on earth than our own dear country. And we're not wrong. The only improvement would be reliable sun for the summer. So, given a few days in a row of balmy weather, we do nothing but ask ourselves why anyone would go anywhere else.

**Usage:** 'That's three days of temperatures touching 20°C. Sure, why would you go on a foreign holiday?'

# Great drying out

*Optimistic outlook.*

When it's not just sunny but a little bit windy too, that's the perfect weather for popping the clothes outside on the washing line. Time it right and you can even get two loads washed and dried in the same day. Housework does not get better than this.

**Usage:** 'There's to be great drying out tomorrow. I'm setting the alarm for 6am to put a wash on.'

# Grand stretch

*Any sunlight after 5pm.*

There's nothing the Irish love more than the winter solstice. Once we finally make it over the hump of 21 December, we eagerly look forward to the extra minutes of daylight each evening. And that's when we start telling each other (over and over) about the 'grand stretch'. We can't help it, it's in our DNA.

**Usage:** 'Middle of January already. Won't be long 'til we see a grand stretch in the evenings.'

CONGRATULATIONS &
COMMISERATIONS

# Fair play!

*Slap on the back.*

A phrase the rest of the world understands as equality and respect for all, the Irish use to congratulate someone on a job well done. Can also be a general catch-all response, e.g., after someone's long and boring story, when you are genuinely at a loss as to what to say: 'Fair play!'

**Usage**: 'I heard you finally managed to pass your driving test. Only the five times, eh? Fair play to you!'

Go on, ya good thing /
Good man yourself /
No better buachaill /
No trouble to ye / Some
woman for one woman

*Approval and respect.*

Words to buoy you up, in preparation or in celebration. These phrases can be used either as praise for something already achieved, or as encouragement that someone believes you've got it in you to do it. Of course, there is potential for any of these to tip into the patronising, but that can surely be said for most Irish turns of phrase.

**Usage:** 'You did well there. No better buachaill!'

# Up, ye boyo

*Go on there, lad.*

Usually addressing a male younger than the speaker, the Irish use this one in a more complimentary way than the other nations who picked it up from us (though 'boyo' can also be used as a reprimand for a cheeky young pup). Often to be heard shouted at a player during a GAA match.

**Usage:** 'Great goal! Up, ye boyo!'

# Jammy /
# Haunted

*Lucky.*

This one may have originated in the French phrase *jamais de guerre*, meaning peaceful and prosperous times, or from the sheer luxury of having jam on your bread. Either way, it's a commonly used adjective in Ireland to mean lucky or fortunate. Cork people have their own word, 'haunted', which means much the same. Spooky.

**Usage:** 'I heard you won the club lotto jackpot, you jammy sod!'

# What's for you won't pass you

*Irish mammy philosophy.*

The homegrown equivalent of *que sera, sera*, meaning whatever will be, will be, and there's not much point in struggling against it. When an Irish mammy lays it on you, she's offering comfort after you've lost out on something — like your childhood sweetheart or your hoped-for Leaving Cert results.

**Usage**: 'Don't you worry, there's someone out there for you. What's for you won't pass you.'

# TERMS OF
# ENDEARMENT

# Oul fella / Oul dear / Oul wan / Oul pair

*The folks.*

Can be used to refer to any random older person but, in context, commonly used to mean a parent. And while it may not sound like the most tender way to talk about the people who brought you into the world, we Irish use 'me oul fella' (Daddy) and 'me oul dear' or 'me oul wan' (Mammy) with great fondness. They're not a bad oul pair.

**Usage:** 'The oul fella nearly killed me for leaving the immersion on.'

# Mot

*Girlfriend.*

Dublin slang pronounced without the final 't'. There are a number of possible origins for this one. The romantics among us like to think that it derives from the Irish-language word *maith* meaning 'good' and that favourite saying of teachers up and down the country, *maith an cailín* or 'good girl'.

**Usage:** 'Can't meet up, lads. Another night out without her and me mot'll kill me.'

# Acushla

*Darling.*

From the Irish word *cuisle* or 'darling', this anglicisation literally means 'pulse' of one's heart — almost as if they're a part of you. Often used when talking to a beloved child, it can also be used when addressing a friend or sweetheart.

**Usage:** 'Hush now, acushla. Time for sleep.'

# Musha

*Awwwww.*

Coming from the Irish word *muise*, meaning 'ah' or well', this is a phrase that expresses pity. While it can be used with affection and tenderness, it is often said sarcastically in response to someone feeling a bit sorry for themselves — the Irish equivalent of playing the world's smallest violin.

**Usage:** 'Got a little sniffle there, have you? Musha.'

# Me oul segotia

*Dear friend.*

This curious phrase is reserved for your oldest and fondest pals, and when you want to introduce a little culture into your discourse. It has a few possible origins, including James Joyce's 'skeowsha'; an anglicised version of the Irish-language greeting *seo dhuitse*; or even the Edwardian Dublin society's 'segocioners'.

**Usage:** 'Great to see you, me oul segotia. Will you join me in a drop of the pure?'

# Chancer / Cute hoor / Divil / Sleeveen

*Shameless rogue.*

A complicated insult, this one. Aimed at someone devious and sneaky, it also implies a certain amount of admiration. Often delivered with a shake of the head or a roll of the eyes, to express resigned exasperation. A 'cute hoor' is a special kind of chancer who showcases their dubious skills in business or politics.

**Usage:** 'That fella's such a sleeveen. Wouldn't trust him as far as I could throw him.'

# Craythur

*Wretch.*

From the Irish word *créatúr* or creature, craythur used to mean poteen or whiskey (as in 'a drop of the craythur' in Joyce's *Finnegan's Wake*). These days, it's more commonly used to refer to someone who elicits pity or sympathy. Often preceded by 'poor' or — if all hope is lost — 'godforsaken'.

**Usage:** 'Ara, would ya look? It was all too much for her. The poor craythur is shook.'

# Dote

*Cutie.*

The verb 'to dote' hails from as far back as Middle English, and while you will often hear the Irish talking about 'doting on someone', we also use the noun 'dote' and adjective 'dotey' for someone who is adorably sweet.

**Usage:** 'Would you look at the wee dote — he's the head of you!'

# Yer man /
# Yer wan

*Indeterminate people.*

A handy way to refer to people you either don't know the name of or just aren't in the mood to use right now. That man or that woman over there, sometimes accompanied by a slight indicative nod of the head or even, if called for, a scathing look.

**Usage:** 'Would you look at yer wan over there. What is she at?'

# Young fella / Young wan

*Young person.*

As with all things, context is everything. These terms usually apply to teenagers or people in their twenties but, depending on the relative age of the speaker, they can refer to someone much older. Also, 'her young fella' can mean her son or her boyfriend, so make sure you pay attention or the conversation could get very confusing.

**Usage:** 'I want you to stay away from that young fella. He's nothing but trouble.'

# Chiseller

*Child.*

This inner-city Dublin slang that featured in James Joyce's *Ulysses* may have slightly unsavoury origins. It is thought to come from 'chisel', which was commonly used in the early 20th century to mean to swindle someone out of money. Not how we like to think of our little darlings these days — most of the time, anyway.

**Usage:** 'Six o'clock and not a chiseller in the house washed.'

COMPLIMENTS

# Beure / Feek / Fine thing / Flah / Lasher / Ride

*One who's easy on the eye.*

In a country filled with silver-tongued devils, it's no surprise the Irish have an array of words to describe someone who's a bit of alright. 'Beure' comes from the old Shelta word for woman, while 'ride', flah' and 'feek' all carry double meanings with doing the dirty deed. Mind how you use them and who you use them with.

**Usage:** 'Did you see yer man who's just moved into No. 20? What a total ride!'

# Great colour

*Anything but pale.*

A tan, even a barely perceptible darkening of the pasty Irish complexion.

**Usage:** 'You must have been off on your holliers. You've a great colour, so you do.'

Class / Daycent /
Deadly / Massive /
Mighty / Savage /
Unreal

*Really good.*

When looking to express enthusiasm about someone or something, we Irish have no shortage of terms. While many of them don't feel intuitively complimentary and have significantly different meanings when used in other contexts, even 'deadly', 'massive' and 'savage' are intended as proper adulation.

**Usage:** 'That film was deadly. And yer wan was savage in it and all.'

# Legend

*High-level flattery.*

Inspired by the likes of Cúchulainn and Fionn Mac Cumhaill, a hero of sorts. A legend can be funny, brave, inspiring, mad or just downright reckless.

**Usage:** 'That point you scored on Sunday, girl – you're a feckin' legend!'

# Dead on /
# Sound / Sound
# as a pound

*One of the good ones.*

The use of 'sound' comes from the phrase 'safe and sound', and along with 'dead on', it is perhaps the best compliment an Irish person can pay you. Friendly, easygoing, and an all-round decent sort, let the word go out that you come highly recommended. Top-notch company.

**Usage**: 'That young wan is pure sound, like.'

# Gas craic

*ALL the fun.*

Diverging from the Middle English word 'crak', we've really made 'craic' our own. Someone who's 'gas craic' is fun to be around, quick with the banter, or up for doing dangerous stunts. As well as a person, this one can also be applied to an event or situation.

**Usage**: 'Did you see yer wan throwing shapes to Joe Dolan on the dancefloor? She's gas craic altogether.'

# Not the worst of them / His brother is worse

*High praise indeed.*

A people who usually see the glass as half full, the Irish are loath to give up completely on even the worst kind of scoundrel. There's always someone worse. There's just got to be.

**Usage:** 'That fella is so mean he'd peel an orange in his pocket. But in fairness, his brother is worse; he still has his Communion money.'

# Doing something for Ireland

*World-class activity.*

When you're not just good at something, you're good enough to represent your country at it. Not normally used to refer to the typical Olympic sports but to much more mundane activities. Can also be used to show a dire need, like hunger or tiredness: 'I could sleep for Ireland!'

**Usage:** 'That lad could talk for Ireland. I honestly thought he'd never stop.'

GOOD TIMES

# Craic is 90 / Deadly buzz

*Pinnacle of fun.*

'The craic is 90' seems to come from the same stable of thought as 'up to 90', where 90 is the highest level attainable — in this case, for the fun. 'Buzz' is similar to 'craic', and when it's not just buzz but 'deadly buzz', that definitely makes for a fantastic time for all. But beware: when delivered deadpan and laden with sarcasm, 'deadly buzz' can also mean its opposite.

**Usage:** 'The place was absolutely jammers last night. The craic was 90!'

# Delira and excira

*Joyous expression.*

Made popular by the legendary radio and tv host Gay Byrne, this is a Dublin version of the phrase 'delighted and excited', used to communicate happiness. For maximum authenticity, should be delivered with a theatrical flourish — la-de-dah!

**Usage:** 'I managed to get tickets to this year's *Toy Show*. Could not be more delira and excira.'

# Happy out

*Utterly content.*

This is when everything is going so well that you're not just happy, not just very happy, but utterly, sublimely happy. It's like you're happy from the inside *out* or happy through*out* your whole body.

**Usage:** 'A night in front of the tv with the remote control to myself? I'm happy out!'

# Suckin' diesel

*Going well.*

Not to be taken literally, this phrase has absolutely nothing to do with inhaling fuel, thankfully. It means that you're making great progress, perhaps after solving a problem or removing an obstacle. Now we're getting somewhere!

**Usage**: 'It was a slow start, but we're absolutely suckin' diesel now.'

# Gallivanting

*Irish hedonism.*

We didn't originate this word — it comes from early 19th century English — but it's another one that we put our own spin on. Originally meaning 'to gad about', the Irish generally use it to mean carefree drinking and flirting. What else?

**Usage:** 'You're off out again? Haven't you had enough gallivanting for one week?'

# Shenanigans

*All kinds of messing.*

Thought to derive from *sionnach*, the Irish word for fox — reputed to be the most sly and devious of our native creatures — 'shenanigans' is a word that originally meant trickery. When the Irish talk about shenanigans these days, they mean high spirits with a healthy dollop of mischief.

**Usage:** 'Granny and Grandad are coming over in a minute. While they're here, none of your shenanigans, now.'

# Acting the maggot

*More messing.*

Fooling around, not taking things seriously. Another phrase beloved of parents up and down the country — there's not a child reared in Ireland that hasn't been known to act the maggot when given the opportunity.

**Usage:** 'Sweet mother of divine, would you ever stop acting the maggot?'

# Jo Maxi

*Wheels for hire.*

Dublin term for a taxi, more than likely derived from the cockney rhyming slang 'Joe Baxi'. Was firmly cemented into Irish culture when used as a tv show title in the late 80s/early 90s. *Jo Maxi* was a programme for teenagers on the short-lived channel Network 2, both named in a blatant attempt to be down with the kids.

**Usage:** 'The craic is mighty. Don't just sit there, hop in a Jo Maxi and get down here!'

# Shift

*Kiss.*

Meaning snog, make out, meet, french, pash or score, this versatile word is commonly used as both a noun and a verb (you can 'shift' someone and also 'have a shift'). But let's face it, it's hardly the most appealing of words and does little to conjure up notions of romance.

**Usage:** 'Did you get the shift last night?'

# Doing a line

*Not what you're thinking.*

Much less drug-related than it sounds, this is an old-fashioned phrase for being in a romantic relationship with someone. While it has fallen out of favour in more recent times, many of us remember our parents using it. And of course, there's doing a line, and then there's doing a *strong* line. Now that's serious.

**Usage:** 'I heard those two are doing a strong line. It'll be wedding bells next.'

# Have a grá for

*Fondness for.*

*Grá* is the Irish word for 'love' and can be used to describe being in love with someone. 'Having a grá for' something is a little more casual and can mean anything from a passion for hurling to a craving for a Tayto sandwich.

**Usage:** 'He says he has a grá for the Irish language. But I think that word's about the extent of his knowledge of it and all.'

## About the Author

Kunak McGann grew up in Drogheda, where she spent her childhood gallivanting and foostering about, and generally making the most of the grand stretch in the evening. No longer a young wan, she now works in publishing and lives in Kildare with her husband, two lively sons and one chilled-out dog.

## Also by Kunak McGann

### Red Rover, Red Rover! Games from an Irish Childhood (That You Can Teach Your Kids)

With easy instructions, handy tips and 'risk' ratings', this book will whisk you back to those carefree days of childhood and, if your creaky old bones are up to it, inspire you to get out with the kids and revel in those games all over again.

## By Kunak McGann
## & Sarah Cassidy

## Find out more at obrien.ie